Number Symbolism for Beginners

Types of Symbolism, Variants, Meanings and Applications

Contact: www.HarryEilenstein.de
Harry.Eilenstein@web.de
Harry Eilenstein at youtube

Production and publishing house: BoD – Books on Demand, Norderstedt

ISBN: 9783753490076

Table of Contents

3

I The four types of number symbolism

Number symbolism is often a rather spongy matter: the interpretation of a number is not always the same; it isn't also always clear when a number has a meaning and when it does not; sometimes number mysticism feels a lot like escaping from the world and a lack of grounding; for some people, paying attention to numbers degenerates into obsessiveness …

There are many reasons not to concern oneself with number symbolism …

But one should be careful when forming a judgment about something, so that one does not throw out the baby with the bathwater. Therefore, a careful consideration of the number symbolism could be beneficial.

The first thing that is noticeable is that in general people do not look at all why a number has a certain meaning. There are four different roots of number symbolism, which also say something about the reliability of the symbolism of a special number.

And some numbers have even several "reliable meanings" …

I 1. The natural number symbolism

There are some numbers which have a well assured meaning, because this meaning is found in such different places as in physics and in astrology. To this kind of numbers belong, for example, polarities, angles, rhythms, and the like.

With these numbers one should be able to assume that they are reliable – in their interpretation in omens, in their application in magic and in their use as an indication of certain qualities in research. These numbers should form the foundation of any reliable number symbolism.

However, only the numbers "1", "2", "3", "4", "6" and "12" have a reliable, natural symbolism – the symbolism of "12" results from the symbolism of "3" and "4", but still has an independent quality.

I 2. The traditional-mythological number symbolism

In mythology often certain numbers develop from other numbers – they have thus a secondary symbolism, which was created only by humans.

This includes e.g. the "9", which follows the "8", which has been the perfect number in almost all ancient cultures – the "9" is therefore the destruction of the "8" and thus the number of death. In later times, the "8" has been replaced by the "12" as the perfect number – which then made "13" the number of death.

In some cultures, such as the Teutons, the multiplication of a number by "100" has been used to represent the greatest in the range to which the number multiplied by "100" belongs. For example, "900" represents the greatest in the realm of "9" – the afterlife goddess ("100") in the realm of the dead ("9"), which is why she sometimes has "900 heads".

In mythology numbers have been used partly like adjectives: The "nine worlds" under the world tree, for example, are simply the one realm of the dead – and not nine different underworlds.

I 3. The system number symbolism

There are quite a number of magical-mythological systems whose elements have been numbered: the cards of the Tarot, the hexagrams of the I Ching, the Sephiroth of the Kabbalistic Tree of Life, the seven classical planets, and so on.

There are also some systems in which each letter has a numerical value, such as in the Jewish Gematria, whereby each word has a certain "sum". According to this system, words with the same letter-number sum also have the same qualities. The most known number from this system is the number "666", which originally was the number of the sun, but in the revelation of John became the number of the enemy of God.

There are also in today's time isolated systematic number symbolisms – e.g. in architecture: "00" means "toilet".

Finally also the different number systems have coined the symbolism of the numbers important for this system:

In the Paleolithic binary system, the 1, the 2, the 4, and the 8 have meaning;

in the decimal system the 10, the 100 and the 1000 have a meaning; and

in the duodecimal system, the 12, the 144, etc. have a meaning.

These numbers are found as symbolism especially in mythology.

I 4. The individual number symbolism

Finally, there is the individual number symbolism. It arises in two ways, which are, however, closely related to each other.

1. If one (like me) was born on 8.8., one will have an associative connection to the "8" – a friend of mine who was born on 9.9.1999 has such a connection to the "9".

The numbers, which have played a formative role in one's own life at some point, go over, so to speak, into the associative image treasure of one's own subconscious and thus become a part of one's own individual symbolism, which can also contain numbers.

2. If one deals more intensively with number symbolism, one will develop a preference for one or the other symbolism – for the Jewish Gematria, for the numbers of the hexagrams of the I Ching, for the numbers of the Tarot cards, for the binary number symbolism from the Old Stone Age, for the Jewish Gematria, for the North Germanic number symbolism, for the numbers of the Maya calendar – there is a rich selection available.

From these two sources then the individual number symbolism feeds itself, on the basis of which one can interpret e.g. "coincidences" as omens or which one can use in magic as an analogy system.

For oneself this individual system is of great importance – but when cooperating with others, however, one must agree on a system which one uses together. Fortunately, there are also some numbers which have the same meaning in several systems.

I 5. Result: different symbolisms

According to the very different derivations of the symbolism of the numbers, especially with the small numbers below 10, now and then a far-reaching uniformity of the symbolism can be found – e.g. because the "2" is in almost every system a pair or an opposite complement.

In particular with the number symbolisms derived from a system, however, very different meanings of the numbers can be found.

II   The application of the number symbolism

First of all, the numbers help in understanding a situation – generally through the numbers with natural properties as well as in omens and oracles through the traditional and systematic meanings of the numbers. Of course, the individual associations to the numbers are of great importance, because they are ultimately the "garment" that any number symbolism wears for the person concerned.

Furthermore the numbers can also help with the orientation within a system, which possesses a number symbolism.
One can also find analogies between two areas on the basis of the numbers.

Finally, the numbers can be used actively in magic – for example, when making talismans and the like.
In occidental magic, number squares with the side length of the respective planet have been derived from the numbers of the planets: Saturn has a number-square of 3·3=9 fields, Jupiter a number-square of 4·4=16 fields, Mars one with 5·5=25 fields etc. up to the moon, to which a number-square with 9·9=81 fields belongs.
The numbers are arranged in these squares in such a way that in each row, column and diagonal the same sum is found. In the square of Saturn there are the numbers from 1 to 9, in that of Jupiter those from 1 to 16, in that of Mars those from 1 to 25 etc. up to that of the Moon with the numbers from 1 to 81.
Using the numerical values of the letters in a word, these words can be represented as lines in a number square: One draws a line from the square containing the number corresponding to the first letter of the word to the square containing the number corresponding to the second letter of the word, and so on.

On the whole, however, number symbolism is used much more often for the interpretation of omens and oracles than for magic.

III The Numbers

The "0"

a) natural symbolism of the "0"

Everything, that is there in the material world, is at least "1", but not "0", because then it would not be there …

So for the "0" only the state before the big bang comes into question – and possibly the black holes (of which one or several are in the center of almost every galaxy) since the space and the time in the black hole are completely cut off from the space and the time in the rest of the universe.

Furthermore the sum of two equaly large opposites is "0".

b) traditional-mythological symbolism of the "0"

The "fool" from the Tarot symbolizes the fool from inexperience, the fool from stupidity and the wise fool.

In Kabbalah, the "0" corresponds roughly to the "Ain Soph Aur" (limitless light) that has been before creation. This concept is also called "the three veils of negative existence". This is similar to the state of the world before the big bang.

c) System symbolism of the "0"

The "0" was invented around 400 B.C. by the Indians in order to be able to write blanks in a number – otherwise one could not have distinguished "1030" and "13". The "0" was also used by the Babylonians (but only rarely) and also by the Egyptians, who wrote the "0" with the hieroglyph for "no, not, nothing".

A symbolism of the "0" is not known from this time.

Today the number "00" symbolizes the "room, that has to be build befor all other rooms": the bathroom, that is not counted among the "numbered rooms". The loo was not thougt of as being worth to have a number …

The "1"

a) natural symbolism of the "1"

The "1" represents naturally the beginning, the source and the origin and is therefore also the number which can symbolize God in a logical way.

Since the consciousness is ultimately a unity, which has separated itself in the individual humans only by the consciousness borders towards the consciousness of other humans, one can symbolize also the consciousness with the "1".

That the unity of the consciousness of all people, living beings and things is really real can be seen by telepathy and telekinesis and also by the existence of the collective subconsciousness.

Gravity is the most original of all forces. It is unipolar, i.e. all matter and all energy attract each other by gravity – gravity makes clear that the world is a unity.

The singularity, that is the big bang, is the clearest "1" in the physical-astronomical world view.

In astrology the 0° angle between two planets is called "conjunction". This aspect is like a marriage, a union, a fusion of the two planets that have a distance of 0°. Because of this the angle of 0° has the symbolism of "1".

In psychology, the oral phase corresponds to the symbolism of "1": The baby lives in a symbiosis with its mother – in a unity. Even more clearly than for the first year of a child's life, this naturally applies to the pregnancy itself.

This phase corresponds to the Paleolithic Age, when people lived in nature as part of nature.

b) traditional-mythological symbolism of the "1"

There is surprisingly little traditional symbolism about the "1" – possibly it simply remains unspoken because it is taken for granted.

This "1" appears, for example, in the sweat lodge mandala in the center as Wakan Tanka ("Great Mystery"), from which all things have sprung and which is the life in all things. In the six directions around the center are to the east the serpent, to the north the bear, to the east the eagle, to the south the buffalo woman, above Grandfather Sky and below Grandmother Earth.

In general, the center of all mandalas is a correspondence to the number "1".

The "Magician" from the Tarot symbolizes initiative and foundation.

The rune "Fehu" symbolizes prosperity, which at that time corresponded to the literal translation of "Fehu": cattle.

The Hebrew letter "Aleph", which stands for the "1", represents a bull's head.

On the Egyptian yardstick ("royal cubit") the "1" is symbolized by the sun-god Re.

c) system symbolism of the "1"

In grammar, the singular is the "1".

In the Kabbalistic Tree of Life, the Sephirah "Kether" is the origin of all things, the underlying unity of everything – God.

The Tao of the Chinese corresponds to the "1": The Tao is the origin of all things.

In the I Ching the hexagram "Ki'en (Chi'en)" has the meaning "Heaven". With it the creative principle is meant.

The "2"

a) natural symbolism of the "2"

The "2" has two clearly distinguishable symbolisms: expansion and opposition.

Expansion

The "2" is the point from which a ray emanates, that is, an expansion. On a large scale, this condition existed in the first 10^{-32} seconds after the Big Bang. This phase is called "inflationary universe", i.e. "inflating universe", because in this short time the universe expanded with 10^{52} times the speed of light to 10^{26} times the size as before. That has been the biggest "explosion" which has ever existed.

Contrast

The second oldest basic force after gravity is the electromagnetic force. It is bipolar, i.e. it occurs as "+" and as "−". Equal poles repel each other, unequal attract each other, the sum of two equal "+" or "−" charges results in "0", i.e. the neutral state.

In astrology, this bipolarity is found in the aspect of opposition, where two planets are at a 180° angle to each other – that is, exactly opposite.

The essence of opposition is the swing, the oscillation, the wave, the back and forth, the change, the rhythm, the cycle …

The most fundamental form of the complementary opposition are the two sides of the world: the inside of consciousness and the outside of matter and energy.
The consciousness is ultimately a unity and therefore free: There is nothing second which could influence the unity.
Matter is a multiplicity and therefore inert, because all parts influence each other: This is the origin of the laws of nature.
So the world is free on the inside and inert on the outside – which is why every human being can be creative.

b) traditional-mythological symbolism of the "2"

The principle of the opposite-complement is found in very many areas.
The oldest variant is probably this world and the hereafter. The Chinese Yin and Yang originally also denoted this world and the hereafter.

Also "consciousness and matter" might be a very old concept – originally probably as "body and soul".

In a sweat lodge, the above represents the responsibility of Grandfather Heaven and the below represents the trust of Grandmother Earth.

The West represents the view at the small through the serpent and the East represents the view at the great through the eagle.

The north embodies egoism and self-assertion by the bear and the south the creation of community and security by the buffalo woman.

A clearly later contrast version is "God and Devil", where the devil should explain the evil in the world.

The "High Priestess" from the Tarot symbolizes silence and meditation.

The rune "Ur" symbolizes the healing.

On the Egyptian yardstick ("royal cubit") the "2" is symbolized by Ma'at, the goddess of accuracy.

The Hebrew letter "Beth", which stands for the "2", represents a house.

The anal phase, which follows the oral phase, is also characterized by an opposition: pleasant – unpleasant; familiar – strange; wanting to have – wanting to avoid, etc.

In the Neolithic period, which corresponds to the anal phase, this opposition appears as the grain god and the wilderness god.

The rhythm of eternal change is found in the Neolithic as the change of seasons in agriculture.

In the anal phase, the rhythm is found in the importance of the regulated, reliable rhythmic daily routine for the child.

c) system symbolism of the "2"

In the grammar of almost all ancient languages, besides the singular and the plural, there was also the dual, that is, the "two number". The dual was used for the eyes, the ears, the arms, the legs, for a pair, for man and woman, for the two panther statues next to the temple entrance and the like. The dual, like the singular and the plural, had its own grammatical ending.

In the Kabbalistic Tree of Life, the Sephirah "Chokmah" is, on the one hand, the uninhibited expansion, the unrestrained self-expression and, on the other hand, the "vision of God face to face".

In the I Ching the hexagram "Kun" has the meaning "earth". It is the passive, receiving.

The number "e"

a) natural symbolism of the number "e"

The number "e" has the magnitude "2.71828182846...". It is the basis of the e-function, i.e. of all growth curves. One should assume that this number appeares in all symbolisms concerning growth and the increase of something.

However, it is not used as a rule for this purpose.

The "3"

a) natural symbolism of the "3"

The "3" has three clearly distinguishable symbolisms: 1. the cohesion, 2. the opposition and its rhythm, and 3. the development.

It is noticeable that the "1" has one single natural symbolism, the "2" has two natural symbolisms, and the "3" has three natural symbolisms.

Cohesion

The third basic force is the strong interaction, which is also called "color force". It is three-polar, i.e. the particles (quarks), from which this force and its mediators (gluons) originates occur in three different qualities, which are called "red", "blue" and "yellow" for illustration. Together these three qualities ("colors") then result in the neutral state – in the color analogy thus "white".

The three quarks are held together in a proton or in a neutron by the gluons so firmly that one cannot separate them. If you try to do this, you have to spend so much energy that this energy eventually turns into three more quarks because of "$E=mc^2$" – whereupon you don't have a single quark, but two quark triads instead of just one …

This quality of cohesion is found in astrology in the trine aspect which connects two planets at an angle of 120°.

In the triclinic crystal lattice the ions are at a distance of 120° from each other. In stone healing, these crystals have the quality of cohesion and integration and therefore of steadfastness and sincerity.

In the beginning of the phallic phase (3 years) the child learns to say "I". Through the security in the oral phase ("Yes") and the distinction and rejection in the anal phase ("No!"), the child has learned to recognize himself as the center of his world and to follow his will ("I!!!").

The child has integrated his psyche – which corresponds completely to the color power and the astrologic trine.

The historical equivalent to the phallic phase is kingship with monotheism and philosophy: everything is directed by one center.

Contrast and Rhythm

The "3" can also be an opposition and the resulting rhythm. The best known of these systems is probably the threefolding of Rudolf Steiner, who used as poles the expansion ("Lucifer") and the contraction ("Arhiman"), from which then a rhythmic system results ("Christ").

This structural principle is also found in some crop circles. These crop circles consist in the center of a large ring in which the energy pulsates.

This circular ring is divided by a straight line into two equal halves. At the two places where this straight line ends at the ring, there is a small circle each – one of them is a circular surface that expands and feels like a mountain; the other of them is a circular ring that contracts and feels like a cave.

These two outer circles are the two poles that make the energy flow and pulsate in the middle, large ring.

Without the large ring, that is, just the two outer circles and the straight line, we get the astrological symbol for oppostion (σ^o). In this context, the great circular ring can be understood as the zodiac in which this astrological aspect is located.

The cool, passive yin and the warm, active yang, together with the constant change, form exactly the same structure, represented as the eternally turning Yin/Yang sign. After these changes ("I") the book "I Ching" has been named: "The book of changes".

Development

All developments proceed in three steps: 1. the uninhibited expansion, 2. the clear structure and 3. the rhythmic contact.

In the zodiac these are the three dynamics in which the four elements appear: 1. cardinal, 2. fixed and 3. mutable.

On the arm, these are 1. the upper arm (general direction), 2. the forearm (local movement), and 3. the hand (contact).

On the leg, these are correspondingly 1. the thigh, 2. lower leg and 3. foot.

In the chakras, this principle is found sixfold:

- 1. solar plexus, 2. hara and 3. root chakra
- 1. throat chakra, 2. third eye and 3. crown chakra
- 1. right upper arm minor chakra, 2. right forearm minor chakra and 3. right hand minor chakra
- 1. left upper arm minor chakra, 2. left forearm minor chakra and 3. left hand minor chakra
- 1. right thigh minor chakra, 2. right lower leg minor chakra and 3. right foot monir chakra
- 1. left thigh minor chakra, 2. left lower leg minor chakra and 3. left foot

minor chakra.

Every business has these three phases: 1. Foundation and expansion, 2. structuring and regimentation, and 3. slow growth and flourishing.

In the psyche, these three phases are found as 1. emotion, 2. thinking and 3. perception.

In the world as a whole, these three phases are found as 1. the free acting consciousness, 2. as the unfolding realm structured by analogies (which becomes visible, for example, as a horoscope), and 3. as the material world shaped by the laws of nature.

The cabbalistic tree of life is a differentiated form of this "three-step":

> 1. the world
> 2. the consciousness (Kether, God), the unfolding and the matter (Malkuth)
> 3. the unfolding is again divided into three phases: God – deities – souls – psyches – matter.
> 4. these three areas of unfoldment are again divided into three phases each: God (Kether) – deities (Chokmah, Binah, Da'ath) – souls (Chesed, Geburah, Tiphareth) – psyches (Netzach, Hod, Yesod) – matter (Malkuth).

A somewhat more static variant of this principle is Hegel's triad "thesis, antithesis, synthesis".

b) traditional-mythological symbolism of the "3"

Saturn is traditionally depicted on a triangle on talismans and the like in Western culture. Thus the Saturn metal "lead" is also associated with the "3".

The sun is represented since the late Paleolithic (or even earlier) as a circular face with three legs (the "skywalker"): the triskelis.

In Christianity, the "3" is found as the Trinity, these three corresponding to the three phases: God the Father, Christ and the Holy Spirit.

The "Empress" from the Tarot symbolizes fertility, flourishing and nature.

The rune "Thorn" symbolizes the sword of the former sungod-father and sword-god Tyr. "Thorn" literally means "thorn."

On the Egyptian yardstick ("royal cubit") the "3" is symbolized by the earthgod Geb.

The Hebrew letter "Gimel", which stands for the "3", represents a camel hump and thus indirectly also a camel.

c) system symbolism of the "3"

The third grammatical form that refers to number, besides the singular and the dual, is the plural. The singular is represented in the ancient Egyptian hieroglyphic writing by a small vertical stroke, the dual by two such strokes and the plural by three strokes.

Because the "3" stands for the plural, the "3" has also developed to a symbol for "many", for "a long series", "for endless repetitions" and finally for "cycle" and thus also for "sun" – the sun is by day/night and summer/winter the most conspicuous example for a cycle.

Therefore, the solar disk as a celestial wanderer in Eurasia has been given three legs.

In the Kabbalistic Tree of Life, the Sephirah "Binah" is cohesion, connectedness and community – and thus the "Great Mother".

In the I Ching, the hexagram "Chun" has the meaning "difficulties at the beginning".

The number "Π"

a) natural symbolism of the number "Π"

The number "Pi" has the size "3.14159265358...". It indicates the ratio between the diameter and the circumference of a circle.

So it would be conceivable to use it as a symbol for roundness, harmony, expansion, cycle and the like – but to my knowledge this is not done.

The "4"

a) natural symbolism of the "4"

The "4" appears as a right angle (90° = 1/4 of a circle) in many places. In physics it can be found most clearly as the always right angle between an electric wave and the corresponding magnetic wave. Both waves reach their maximum and minimum alternately. The square separates these two waves.

In astrology, the square aspect separates two planets that are 90° apart. It separates them, but at the same time it relates them to each other: the astrological square is like a tent pole that separates the floor canvas and the ceiling canvas, thus creating a space.

The same property is found in stone healing with the cubic crystal lattice: stones with this crystallization form create space, delimit, establish order, help in self-defense, etc.

b) traditional-mythological symbolism of the "4"

The four points of the compass have resulted from the sunrise point, the midday point, the sunset point and the midnight point in a hardly avoidable, natural way.
The "4" of the cardinal points has therefore also the meaning "everywhere".
The sun as that with whose help one can recognize the four cardinal points was also symbolized itself as a circle (horizon) with a cross in it (four directions). To indicate the turning of the sun, the four "spokes" of this "wheel" were bent a little, creating the swastika: the "bent cross".

Jupiter is traditionally depicted in Western culture on talismans and the like on a square. Thus, the Jupiter metal "tin" is also associated with the "4".

The "Emperor" from the tarot symbolizes dominion.

The rune "Ansus" symbolizes the Aesir, the gods of the Germanic tribes.

On the Egyptian yardstick ("royal cubit") the "4" is symbolized by Nut, the goddess of heaven.

The Hebrew letter "Daleth", which stands for the "4", represents an opened tent door.

c) system symbolism of the "4"

In the Kabbalistic Tree of Life, the Sephirah "Chesed" is the highest area where there are independent beings – thus the soul with its memory of its previous incarnations is found here. In this area one can find all information – all. Therefore this "place" is also called "Akasha-Chronik" and the like.

In the I Ching the hexagram "Meng" has the meaning "Youth".

The "5"

a) natural symbolism of the "5"

The astrological aspect Quincunx belongs to the "5", because it has the size of 5/12 of a circle, thus 150°. The "5" has the dynamics of the quincunx, that is, the constant renewal and transformation by integrating what is happening at the moment.

The "5" is the smallest integer size of the hypotenuse in the Pythagorean theorem: In a right triangle, if the minor cathetus measures 3cm and the major cathete measures 4cm, then the hypotenuse measures 5cm ($3^2+4^2=5^2 \Rightarrow 9+16=25$).

There are a number of places where the "5" occurs in nature, but they are all not as fundamental as, for example, those where the numbers "1" to "4" occurred:

- There are 5 platonic bodies.

- Almost all vertebrates have 5 fingers or toes.

- The starfish and its relatives have 5 arms.

- Many plants have five-petaled flowers and correspondingly five-part fruits (which becomes visible if you cut the fruit horizontally).

One has the impression that the "5" still belongs to the numbers with a natural symbolism, but that this symbolism is a little "stubborn" and not so easily tangible. This would also correspond to the character of the astrological quincunx, which cannot be "nailed down", so to speak, but which describes a relationship between two planets that is in constant transformation.

b) traditional-mythological symbolism of the "5"

Mars is traditionally depicted in western culture on talismans and the like on a pentagon. Thus also the Mars metal "iron" is associated with the "5".

In Asia there are the 5 elements fire, water, air, metal and wood.

The pentagram is considered to be the four elements plus the quintessence ("fifth elemen"t). The top of the pentagram is often seen as the head of the human being, the two middle points as his arms and the two lower points as his legs.

The pentagram with one point upwards symbolizes the dominion of spirit over matter and thus God – the pentagram with one point down symbolizes the dominion of matter over spirit and thus the devil. This is, of course, a very specific, polarized view of the world that one does not necessarily have to share.

The "High Priest" from the Tarot symbolizes knowledge, cult and magic.

The rune "Reid" symbolizes the ride and therefore in general the journey, the wandering and the ride with the dragon ship.

On the Egyptian yardstick ("royal cubit") the "5" is symbolized by the grain god Osiris.

The Hebrew letter "He", which stands for the "5", represents a person with raised hands rejoicing or calling upon God.

This corresponds to the high priest and partly also to the pentagram and the god Osiris.

c) system symbolism of the "5"

In the Kabbalistic Tree of Life, the Sephirah "Geburah" embodies kinship and development and thus also the realm of karma. In Christian mythology this area corresponds to purgatory.

In the I Ching the hexagram "Hsu" has the meaning "waiting", but also "nourishment".

The "6"

a) natural symbolism of the "6"

The "6" and the 60° angle belonging to it (1/6 of 360°) appear everywhere where many equal elements join together to form a group:

     - spheres in a bucket
     - protons and neutrons in an atomic nucleus
     - several moons in the same orbit around a planet
     - ions in a hexagonal crystal lattice
     - water molecules in a snowflake
     - honeycombs in a beeswax
       etc.

This corresponds to the essence of the astrological sextile aspect, which connects two planets that are 60° apart: the forming of a group.

b) traditional-mythological symbolism of "6"

In Western culture, the Sun is traditionally represented on talismans and the like on a hexagon (honeycomb, hexagon). Thus also the sun-metal "gold" is associated with the "6".

The "lovers" from the tarot symbolize "love", but also "decision".

The rune "Kaun" symbolizes fever and therefore also protection against illness.

On the Egyptian yardstick ("royal cubit") the "6" is symbolized by the mother-goddess Isis.

The Hebrew letter "Vau", which stands for the "6", represents a hook.

c) system symbolism of the "6"

In the Kabbalistic Tree of Life, the Sephirah "Tiphareth" is the soul with its intention for its current incarnation. This is the aspect of one's soul that one finds first when embarking on the journey to one's center.

In the I Ching, the hexagram "Sung" has the meaning of "dispute, strife, conflict".

The "7"

b) traditional-mythological symbolism of the "7"

Venus is traditionally depicted in Western culture on talismans and the like on a heptagon. Thus also the Venus metal "copper" is associated with the "7".

Since there are seven planets visible to the naked eye (Moon, Mercury, Venus, Sun, Mars, Jupiter, Saturn) the "7" early became a number that represented a "complete group of different beings or elements".

The "chariot" (victory chariot) from the Tarot symbolizes drive, enterprise, conquest, and the like.

The rune "Hagal" symbolizes hail and in the figurative sense also the "hail of battle", i.e. spears and arrows.

On the Egyptian yardstick ("royal cubit") the "7" is symbolized by the jackal god Anubis, who is also the archetype of the funeral priests.

The Hebrew letter "Zajin", which stands for the "7", represents a sword.

c) system symbolism of the "7"

In the Kabbalistic Tree of Life, the Sephirah "Netzach" is the realm of impulses and feelings.

In the I Ching the hexagram "Shih" has the meaning "army" and therefore secondarily also "battle, competition, business".

The "8"

b) traditional-mythological symbolism of the "8"

In the Old Stone Age binary number system there were only the numbers "1", "2", "4" and "8". With them one could represent all numbers, which one needed precisely – thus the numbers up to 15: "8+4+2+1". The "9" is in this system an "8+1" and the "11" is an "8+2+1".

The "8" as the "greatest number" became the "round number" and finally the "perfect number". Therefore it was associated with the sun which cannot be influenced by anything. In addition, the four cardinal points together with the four intermediate directions also resulted in "8" – and the cardinal points could only be recognized by the position of the sun (until the invention of the compass), whereby the cardinal points have been closely associated with the sun.

The octagon as the basic form of architecture in the Romanesque period is also based on this symbolism.

In Western culture, Mercury is traditionally depicted on talismans and the like on an octagon. Thus also the Mercury quicksilver (sometimes substituted by brass) is associated with the "8".

The "Justice" from the Tarot represents justice – "Justitia". It is closely associated with balance and equilibrium, which are basic elements of justice.

The rune "Naut" symbolizes the sea and distress – but not only the distress of sailors.

On the Egyptian yardstick ("royal cubit") the "8" is symbolized by the mother-goddess Nephthys.

The Hebrew letter "Chet, which stands for the "8", represents a fence or a similar obstacle.

c) system symbolism of the "8"

In the Kabbalistic Tree of Life, the Sephirah "Hod" is the realm of thoughts and structures.

In the I Ching, the hexagram "Pi " has the meaning of "harmony, cooperation, union".

The "9"

b) traditional-mythological symbolism of the "9"

As a step that follows the perfection of the "8", the "9" can only be the destruction and death. After the "12" took over the symbolism of the "8", the "13" moved to the place of the "9" and its afterlife symbolism.

The moon is traditionally depicted on talismans and the like in Western culture on a nine-corner. Thus also the moon metal "silver" is associated with the "9".

The "hermit" from the Tarot symbolizes retreat, reflection, contemplation, research etc. – which fits quite good to the beyond symbolism of the "9".

The rune "Is" symbolizes ice.

On the Egyptian yardstick ("royal cubit") the "9" is symbolized by the falcon-god Horus, who is the archetype of the soul bird.

The Hebrew letter "Tet", which stands for the "9", represents a wheel.

c) system symbolism of the "9"

In the Kabbalistic Tree of Life, the Sephirah "Yesod" is the realm of perceptions and memories.

In the I Ching, the hexagram "Hsioa Ch'u" has the meaning "the taming of the small forces": calm, restraint, preparation.

The Ba-Gua in Feng-Shui has $3 \cdot 3 = 9$ fields – but the Ba-Gua is not usually associated with the "9".

The "10"

b) traditional-mythological symbolism of the "10"

The "10" is sometimes associated with the earth as a planet and as the ground under our feet. As a symbol, two combined pentagrams appear now and then, one pointing up and the other pointing down: a ten-pointed star.

The "wheel of life" (wheel of destiny) from the tarot symbolizes the ups and downs of life.

The rune "Algiz" symbolizes the elk and, by extension, the deer.

The Hebrew letter "Jod", which stands for "10", represents a hand.

c) system symbolism of the "10"

In the Kabbalistic Tree of Life, the Sephirah "Malkuth" is the realm of the body and matter in general.

In the I Ching the hexagram "Lu" has the meaning "the appearance". Through it one can receive advice.

The "11"

b) traditional-mythological symbolism of the "11"

The "Strength" from the Tarot symbolizes strength and self-control.

The rune "Sol" symbolizes the sun.

c) system symbolism of the "11"

In the I Ching the hexagram "T'ai" has the meaning "the peace" and therefore secondarily also "prosperity, flourishing, harmony".

The "12"

a) natural symbolism of the "12"

the 12-divided circle

The current physical theory used to describe the world is the superstring theory. A superstring is a circle that vibrates like a string with a standing wave. This superstring can be pictured as a string that has been stretched into a circle. On this superstring there are 12 points at a distance of 30°, which are always at rest. The areas in between oscillate alternately up and down. Thus, there are 12 sharply defined areas on this string.

The superstrings were originally called "Heisenberg's spin chains" after their discoverer.

The zodiac has exactly the same structure: 12 zodiacal signs of 30° length, which are sharply delimited from each other.

The three sections of the 12 parts

Such a 30° section on a superstring oscillates highest in its center and much flatter at its two ends – the oscillation is a sine curve.

The differently strong oscillation on the 12 delimited sections of the super-string correspond to the three 10°-sections of each sign of the zodiac, which differ slightly in their quality.

the 3·4=12 parts

There are 12 basic elementary particles in physics. They are a group of four particles (up-quark, down-quark, electron, neutrino) that come in three different sizes.

In astrology, this corresponds to the four elements (fire, water, air, earth), which occur in three different dynamics (cardinal, fixed, mutable).

the platonic bodies

The symbolism of the "12" as the smallest unit resting in itself (elementary particles, zodiac) results from the combination (i.e. multiplication) of the cohesion of the "3" and the spatial expansion of the "4". In the "12" are also found the identity of the "1", the complementary opposition of the "2" and the group formation of the "3".

The "12" summarizes therefore all known natural number symbols and creates from them the "consistent form".

Interestingly, these numbers are also found in the surfaces of the five Platonic solids, which consist of only one kind of equilateral surfaces (triangle, square, pentagon, hexagon = honeycomb):

- Tetrahedron (triangular pyramid): 4 equilateral triangles (3)
- Hexahedron (cube): 6 squares (4)
- Octahedron: 8 triangles (3)
- Dodecahedron: 12 pentagons (5)
- Icosahedron: 20 triangles (3)

You can add the three shapes from which you can form surfaces:

- triangles (3)
- squares (4)
- hexagons = honeycombs (6)

The point has the number "1" and the line the number "2" (two ends).

In the following overview, the natural symbol numbers are highlighted in darker gray:

natural symbol numbers and platonic solids					
platonic solids and surfaces of equal shapes as well as point and line	number of corners	number of edges	number of surfaces	number of corners of surfaces	number of surfaces that meet at a corner
Triangle-pyramid	4	6	4	3	3
Cube	8	12	6	4	3
Pentagon dodecahedron	20	30	12	5	3
Triangle octahedron	6	12	8	3	4
Triangle icosahedron	12	30	20	3	5
Triangle area	-	-	-	3	6
Square area	-	-	-	4	4
Honeycomb area	-	-	-	6	3
Line	-	-	-	2	1
Point	-	-	-	1	-

The possible numbers of the corners of the individual surfaces (3, 4, 5, 6) as well as the possible numbers of the surfaces which meet at a corner (3, 4, 5, 6) are the same and are besides all numbers with a natural symbolism.

The remaining numbers in this overview (8, 20, 30) result from simple multiplications of numbers with natural symbolism: $2 \cdot 4 = 8$; $4 \cdot 5 = 20$; $6 \cdot 5 = 30$.

This consideration strengthens the impression that the "5" belongs to the numbers with a natural symbolism.

The natural symbolic numbers

All these natural symbolic numbers are found as astrological aspects. These seven aspects represent the possible distances between two signs of the zodiac. Since there are 12 zodiac signs and the circle has 360°, each zodiac sign has a length of 30°. Therefore the possible aspects are a multiple of 30°.

the astrological aspects				
Name	*Size in X°*	*magnitude as fraction*	*Symbol number*	*Quality*
conjunction	$0 \cdot 30° = \quad 0°$	same place	1	unity
opposition	$6 \cdot 30° = 180°$	half circle	2	opposition
trine	$4 \cdot 30° = 120°$	1/3 circle	3	connection
square	$3 \cdot 30° = \quad 90°$	1/4 circle	4	separation
quincunx	$5 \cdot 30° = 150°$	5/12-Kreis	5	processing
sextile	$2 \cdot 30° = \quad 60°$	1/6 circle	6	contact
semisextile	$1 \cdot 30° = \quad 30°$	1/12 circle	12	evolution

The natural symbol numbers are thus derived from the zodiac and from the superstring, which are both a circle with a division into 12 equal parts. The zodiac and the superstring are the same structure on the consciousness-inside of the world (zodiac) and on the matter-outside of the world (superstring).

Since all things contain this 12-structure as a basic building block, all things are also characterized by the quality of the "12" as well as the numbers "1", "2", "3", "4", "5" and "6" contained in it. These are therefore the seven natural symbolic numbers.

b) traditional-mythological symbolism of the "12"

The 12 signs of the zodiac have inspired many groups of 12: the 12 gods on Olympus, the 12 gods in Asgard, the 12 apostles, etc.

The "Hanged Man" from the Tarot symbolizes self-sacrifice, devotion, the fever of healing, therapy, the otherworld journey, etc.

The rune "Tyr" symbolizes the original sungod-godfather of the Teutons, who traveled as a sungod through the underworld every night.

Among the Teutons, one became an adult at the age of 12 and could then command a dragon ship, for example.

c) system symbolism of the "12"

In the I Ching the hexagram "P'i" has the meaning "stagnation" and therefore also "poverty, hard times".

The "13"

b) traditional-mythological symbolism of the "13"

The "13" is one step bigger than the "12". Since the "12" is the perfect number, this step out of the "12" is the destruction of perfection and therefore death.

The "Death" from the Tarot symbolizes death and generally all kinds of transformations.

The rune "Biarka" symbolizes the birch tree.

c) system symbolism of the "13"

In the I Ching, the hexagram "T'ung Jen" has the meaning "the brotherhood of man": unification, cooperation, a group with a common goal".

The "14"

b) traditional-mythological symbolism of the "14"

The "14" is in rare cases a half lunar cycle of 28 days.

The "Temperance" from the Tarot symbolizes the right measure.

The rune "Man" symbolizes Mannus, the ancestor of man.

On the Egyptian yardstick ("royal cubit") the "14" is symbolized by the ibis-god Thot, who is the god of writing and wisdom.

c) system symbolism of the "14"

In the I Ching, the hexagram "Ta Yu" has the meaning "the great possession": wealth, prosperity, success.

The "15"

b) traditional-mythological symbolism of the "15"

The "Devil" from the Tarot symbolizes the repressed, the shadow, the feared and of course the devil.

The rune "Lögr" symbolizes water (English: lake).

c) system symbolism of the "15"

In the I Ching the hexagram "Ch'ien" has the meaning "modesty".

The "16"

b) traditional-mythological symbolism of the "16"

In the Tarot there are 16 court cards (kings, queens, knights and squires). However, this derivation of the "16" is almost never used as symbolism.

The "Tower" from the Tarot symbolizes sudden destruction ("the Tower of Babylon").

The rune "Yr" symbolizes the yew tree.

c) system symbolism of the "16"

The "16" is the doubling of the "8" and also a number in the binary system. It therefore occasionally shares the symbolism of completeness and perfection of the "8".

In the I Ching, the hexagram "Yu" has the meaning "bliss" and also the meaning "preparation, enthusiasm".

The Ifa oracle from West Africa is based on an area of $16 \cdot 16 = 256$ fields (see also the symbolism of the "64").

The "17"

b) traditional-mythological symbolism of the "17"

The "star" from the tarot symbolizes goals, wishes and ideals as well as wishful dreams.

The rune "Ehwaz" symbolizes the horse.

c) system symbolism of the "17"

In the I Ching the hexagram "Sui" has the meaning "the consequence": an approach.

The "18"

b) traditional-mythological symbolism of the "18"

The "Moon" from the Tarot symbolizes dreams, the subconscious, the underworld and everything hidden.

The rune "Gifu" symbolizes a gift, a present.

c) system symbolism of the "18"

In the I Ching the hexagram "Ku" has the meaning "the work after the damage".

The orbit of the lunar node lasts approx. 18 years, which is why the "18" can sometimes have the symbolism of a "greater change".

The "19"

b) traditional-mythological symbolism of the "19"

The "Sun" from the Tarot symbolizes the center, the radiance, the self and of course the Sun itself.

c) system symbolism of the "19"

In the I Ching the hexagram "Lin" has the meaning "the approach".

The "20"

b) traditional-mythological symbolism of the "20"

The "Resurrection" from the Tarot symbolizes a healing, a regeneration, a repair and the resurrection, and also an astral journey.

The Hebrew letter "Kaph", which stands for the "20", symbolizes a palm.

c) system symbolism of the "20"

In the I Ching the hexagram "Kuan" has the meaning "the observation".

With the Teutons the "20" is sometimes a "big "2"".

The "21"

b) traditional-mythological symbolism of the "21"

The "world" from the Tarot symbolizes the whole world and also the completeness of a person or a thing, as well as the rhythm of the dance of life.

c) system symbolism of the "21"

In the I Ching, the hexagram "Shih Ho" has the meaning "the chewing": justice, quarrels, obstacles.

The "22"

c) system symbolism of the "22"

In the I Ching the hexagram "Pi" has the meaning "the grace": the adornment, beauty.

Among the Germanic people the "22" is sometimes a "big 2".

The "23"

c) system symbolism of the "23"

In the I Ching the hexagram "Po" has the meaning "the decay".

On the Egyptian yardstick ("royal cubit") the "23" is symbolized a star, the symbol of the soul.

The "24"

c) system symbolism of "24"

In the I Ching, the hexagram "Fu" has the meaning "the return" and also "the revival".

Sometimes the "24" is seen as the "great 12" or a pair of two "12"s – specifically, the 12 hours of the day and the 12 hours of the night, which together make the day. Sometimes 12 gods and 12 goddesses also appear as the core of a pantheon.

The "25"

c) system symbolism of the "25"

In the I Ching the hexagram "Wu Wang" has the meaning "the unexpected" or also "innocence", with which a spontaneity without any calculation is meant.

The symbolism of a "quarter of a hundred", which one could actually expect, does not seem to exist.

The "26"

c) system symbolism of the "26"

In the I Ching, the hexagram "Ta Ch'u" has the meaning "the taming of the great forces": concentration on a great undertaking.

The "27"

c) system symbolism of the "27"

In the I Ching, the hexagram "I" has the meaning "nourishment".

The "28"

b) traditional-mythological symbolism of the "28"

The "28" often refers to the lunar cycle of 28 days, that is, the duration from one full moon to the next full moon (the "28" is not quite precise in this context). The duration of a month, whose name is derived from "moon", is also derived from this symbolism.

c) system symbolism of the "28"

In the I Ching the hexagram "Ta Kuo" has the meaning "the great excess", by which among other things also something extraordinary is meant.

The "29"

c) system symbolism of the "29"

In the I Ching the hexagram "K'an" has the meaning "water", with which "danger, misfortune, a difficult situation" is associated.

The "30"

b) traditional-mythological symbolism of the "30"

The Hebrew letter "Lamed", which stands for the "30", means "exercise, teaching".

c) system symbolism of the "30"

When the term "month", which originated from a time calculation oriented to the moon, was inserted into the time calculation oriented to the course of the sun, it was enlarged to from 28 to 30 days. To the $12 \cdot 30 = 360$ days then five leap days were added, which were attached later on to five of the months, so that some of them received 31 days.

The signs of the zodiac are each 30° long.

In the I Ching the hexagram "Li" has the meaning "the fire" and also "sun, shine, brightness".

The "31"

c) system symbolism of the "31"

In the I Ching the hexagram "Hsien" has the meaning "attraction, stimulation, affection" but also "sensitivity".

The "32"

c) system symbolism of the "32"

In the I Ching, the hexagram "Heng" has the meaning "duration".

The "33"

c) system symbolism of "33"

In the I Ching the hexagram "Tun" has the meaning "retreat", which can also mean "retirement".

With the Teutons the "33" is sometimes a "big 3".

The "34"

c) system symbolism of the "34"

In the I Ching, the hexagram "Ta Chuang" has the meaning "the great power".

The "35"

c) system symbolism of "35"

In the I Ching, the hexagram "Chin" has the meaning "the progress": departure, dawn, sunrise.

The "36

c) system symbolism of the "36"

In the I Ching the hexagram "Ming I" has the meaning "the darkening of the light", thus among other things the night.

The "37

c) system symbolism of the "37"

In the I Ching the hexagram "Chia Jen" has the meaning "the family" and therefore also "responsibility".

The "38"

c) system symbolism of the "38"

In the I Ching the hexagram "K'uei" has the meaning "opposition, struggle, contradiction".

The "39

c) system symbolism of the "39"

In the I Ching, the hexagram "Chien" has the meaning "obstruction", implying difficulty and danger.

The "40"

b) traditional-mythological symbolism of the "40"

The number of 40 cards of the number cards (the four elements from 1 to 10) in the Tarot, strangely enough, has not developed an independent symbolism.

The Hebrew letter "Mem", which stands for the "40", represents an owl.

In the Old Tesatament there has been the tradition of a 40 days long praying, meditating and fasting

c) system symbolism of the "40"

In the I Ching the hexagram "Hsieh" has the meaning "liberation".

Among the Germanic peoples the "40" is sometimes a "big 4". For unclear reasons the "40" appears with the Teutons also as number of the hereafter – maybe in the sense of "behind (=10) the horizon (=4)".

The "41"

c) system symbolism of the "41"

In the I Ching the hexagram "Sun" has the meaning "the reduction": decrease, loss.

The "42"

c) system symbolism of "42"

In the I Ching, the hexagram "I" has the meaning "the increase" and therefore also "advantages, benefits".

The "43"

c) system symbolism of the "43"

In the I Ching, the hexagram "Kuai" has the meaning "determination", which includes "decision".

The "44"

c) system symbolism of the "44"

In the I Ching the hexagram "Kou" has the meaning "the coming together" and secondarily also "friendships, new circumstances".

With the Teutons the "44" is sometimes a "big 4".

The "45"

c) system symbolism "45"

In the I Ching, the hexagram "Ts'ui" has the meaning "the gathering": Celebration, party, ritual, meeting.

The "46"

c) system symbolism of the "46"

In the I Ching, the hexagram "Sheng" has the meaning "the rising": promotion, expansion, the growth of plants.

The "47"

c) system symbolism of the "47"

In the I Ching the hexagram "K'un" has the meaning "distress, confinement".

The "48"

c) system symbolism of the "48"

In the I Ching the hexagram "Ching" has the meaning "well".

The "49"

c) system symbolism of the "49"

In the I Ching the hexagram "Ko" has the meaning "revolution": reform, renewal, overthrow, change.

The "50"

b) traditional-mythological symbolism of the "50"

The Hebrew letter "Nun", which stands for the "50", represents a snake or water.

The symbolism of a "half of a hundred", which one might expect, does not seem to exist.

c) system symbolism of the "50"

In the I Ching the hexagram "Ting" has the meaning "cauldron".

With the Teutons the "50" is sometimes a "big 5".

The "51"

c) system symbolism of the "51"

In the I Ching, the hexagram "Chen" has the meaning "thunder", which also means "shock, awakening, threat, fear, shaking".

The "52"

b) traditional-mythological symbolism of the "52"

The number of 52 weeks in the year does not seem to have developed an independent symbolism.

c) system symbolism of the "52"

In the I Ching, the hexagram "Ken" has the meaning "silence", which is also a reference to meditation.

The "53"

c) system symbolism of the "53"

In the I Ching, the hexagram "Chien" has the meaning "the gradual development": improvement, accretion.

The "54"

b) traditional-mythological symbolism of the "54"

Among the Germanic people, the "54" is the only case of a "reduced number" – it was considered as a reduced "540". Since the "540" was the number of the former sun-god, father of the gods and swordgod Tyr, the "54" could be understood as the number of the sword of Tyr.

However, it is not quite sure whether this "54" was a symbolism or just a riddle in a poem …

c) system symbolism of the "54"

In the I Ching the hexagram "Luei Mei" has the meaning "the marrying girl" and therefore also "marriage, fulfillment, bearing fruit, final decision".

The "55"

c) system symbolism of the "55"

In the I Ching the hexagram "Feng" has the meaning "greatness".

The "56"

b) traditional-mythological symbolism of "56"

The number of 56 cards of the Minor Arcana in the Tarot (40 number cards and 16 court cards) has not developed its own symbolism.

c) system symbolism of the "56"

In the I Ching the hexagram "Lu" has the meaning "the exiled" and from it also "stranger, traveling, wandering".

The "57"

c) system symbolism of the "57"

In the I Ching the hexagram "Sun" has the meaning "wind, carrying out", but also "forest, penetration".

The "58"

c) system symbolism of the "58"

In the I Ching, the hexagram "Tui" has the meaning "joy" and also "happiness, bliss, beauty".

The "59"

c) system symbolism of the "59"

In the I Ching the hexagram "Huan" has the meaning "the dispersion": dissolution, separation.

The "60"

b) traditional-mythological symbolism of the "60"

The Hebrew letter "Samech", which stands for the "60", represents a pillar.

c) system symbolism of the "60"

In the I Ching, the hexagram "Chieh" has the meaning "the restriction", which also includes "surveillance" and "thrift".

With the Teutons the "60" is sometimes a "big 6".

The "61"

c) system symbolism of the "61"

In the I Ching, the hexagram "Chung Fu" has the meaning "inner truthfulness" as well as "sincerity, trust" and "he whom others trust".

The "62"

c) system symbolism of the "62"

In the I Ching, the hexagram "Hsiao Kup" has the meaning "the little excess". This hexagram can also be an indication of a small error with possibly great effect.

The "63"

c) system symbolism of the "63"

In the I Ching, the hexagram "Chi Chi" has the meaning "completion" or "successful, happy conclusion".

The "64"

c) system symbolism of the "64"

In the I Ching, the hexagram "Wei Chi" has the meaning "before completion" and also indicates a period of great effort or concentration before this completion.

The "64" is belongs to the binary numbers (1, 2, 4, 8, 16, 32, 64 ...) and therefore can also have the symbolism of perfection. The hexagrams of the I Ching are arranged on a field of $8 \cdot 8 = 64$ squares. This field is the basis for the chess board and the checkers board. The game of Go with its $19 \cdot 19 = 361$ squares is probably an enlargement of the chess board.

The "70"

b) traditional-mythological symbolism of the "70"

The Hebrew letter "Ajin" (Ayn), which stands for the "70", represents an eye.

c) system symbolism of the "70"

Among the Germanic peoples, the "70" is sometimes a "big 7".

The "77"

c) system symbolism of the "77"

With the Teutons the "77" is sometimes a "big 7".

The "80"

b) traditional-mythological symbolism of the "80"

The Hebrew letter "Pe", which stands for the "80", represents a mouth.

c) system symbolism of the "80"

Among the Germanic peoples, the "80" is sometimes a "big 8".

The "88"

c) system symbolism of the "80"

Among the Teutons, the "88" is sometimes a "big 8".

The "90"

b) traditional-mythological symbolism of the "90"

The Hebrew letter "Tzade" (Tzadi), which stands for the "90", represents a papyrus or generally a plant. Tzade is sometimes also understood as a harpoon.

c) system symbolism of the "90"

Among the Germanic peoples, the "90" is sometimes a "big 9".

The "99"

c) system symbolism of the "99"

With the Teutons the "99" is sometimes a "big 9".

The "100"

b) traditional-mythological symbolism of the "100"

In the decimal system, the "100" has the association "many".

The Hebrew letter "Koph" (Sophia), which represents the "100", represents a monkey.

c) system symbolism of the "100"

Among the Germanic people the "100" has two meanings: on the one hand the great age of a person (100 years) and on the other hand the greatest in a realm – for example "900" is the number of the goddess of the afterlife, thus the greatest ("100") in the realm of the "9" i.e. in the realm of the underworld.

The "108"

b) traditional-mythological symbolism of the "108"

The symbolism of the "108" results from an old Indo-Germanic "number game": $1 \cdot 2 \cdot 2 \cdot 3 \cdot 3 = 108$ or written differently $1^1 \cdot 2^2 \cdot 3^3 = 108$. Here obviously the three most important symbolic numbers were summarized.

Since the "108" always appears in connection with the sun or the sun god, the "108" is probably to be understood as "the one sun god who wanders through the two worlds".

The "1" is "the one sun god"; the "2" is "the two worlds", i.e. the day-world and the night-otherworld; and the "3" is the wandering of the sun, which was represented in the Neolithic Age in Europe and Asia as a sun disk with three legs (triskelis).

From this symbolism derives e.g. in India the 108-times speaking or chanting of a Mantra.

The "200"

b) traditional-mythological symbolism of the "200"

The Hebrew letter "Resch", which stands for the "200", represents a head.

c) system symbolism of the "200"

Among the Germanic peoples, the "200" is sometimes "the largest in the range of 2".

The "256"

c) system symbolism of the "256"

In West Africa, the "256" is the number of fields of the Ifa oracle, which has $16 \cdot 16 = 256$ fields. "256" is a binary number (1, 2, 4, 8, 16, 32, 64, 128, 256 ...).

The "300"

b) traditional-mythological symbolism of the "300"

The Hebrew letter "Shin", which stands for the "300", represents a tooth.

c) system symbolism of the "300"

Among the Germanic people, the "300" is sometimes "the largest in the range of 3". Mostly, however, "endless cycle (3) of lives (100)" is meant, i.e. the course of the sun and thus the endless lives and deaths of the sungod-godfather Tyr. This is a quite popular symbolism in German mythology.

The "360"

b) traditional-mythological symbolism of the "360"

The year was originally counted as 12 months of 30 days each. Then 5 additional days were added to reach the actual year length of 365 days. Since it is more exactly 365.25 days, every four years a leap day is added – which today is February 29.

From these $12 \cdot 30 = 360$ days of the year circle also the division of the circle into 360° was derived.

The "360" symbolizes therefore something round, whole, cyclic.

The "361"

c) system symbolism of the "360"

The $19 \cdot 19 = 361$ squares of the game of Go will probably evoke an association only in Asia.

The "365"

b) traditional-mythological symbolism of the "365"

The "365" is firmly associated with the number of days in the year and therefore with the year itself.

The "400"

b) traditional-mythological symbolism of the "400"

The Hebrew letter "Taw" (Tau), which stands for the "400", represents a cross or star. It is also used to mark an ending, like a dot at the end of a sentence. The "Tau" is therefore also a completion symbol.

c) system symbolism of the "400"

Among the Germanic people, the "400" is sometimes "the largest in the range of 4".

The "500"

b) traditional-mythological symbolism of the "500"

The Hebrew letter "Kaph", which stands for the "500", represents a palm. It is also the symbol for the "20".

c) system symbolism of the "500"

Among the Germanic people, the "500" is sometimes "the largest in the range of 5".

The "540"

b) traditional-mythological symbolism of the "540"

From the solar number "108" of the Indo-Germans, the Germanic tribes derived the number of gates of the hall of the sungod-godfather Tyr by multiplication with "5". This hall of Tyr was later adopted by Odin and Thor. Unfortunately, the meaning of "5" in this context is unclear. Is perhaps according to the pentagram symbolism "dominion" meant? However, the pentagram does not appear as a symbol with the Teutons.

From this "540" of the swordgod Tyr the "54" has been derived as the symbolic number of the sword of Tyr.

The "600"

b) traditional-mythological symbolism of the "600"

The Hebrew letter "Mem" represents an owl. "Mem" actually has the numerical value "40", but is also used to write the "600".

c) system symbolism of the "600"

Among the Germanic peoples, the "600" is sometimes "the largest in the range of 6".

The "666"

b) traditional-mythological symbolism of the "666"

The number "666" is known mainly from the Revelation of John. As a multiple of "6", it was originally a solar number, but has been reinterpreted to the adversary of God or Christ (who were both often compared to the sun).

Probably this is in the Christian area the most well-known symbol number.

The "700"

b) traditional-mythological symbolism of the "700"

The Hebrew letter "Nun" represents water or a snake. The letter "Nun" is actually associated with the number "50", but it is also used secondarily to spell "700".

c) system symbolism of the "700"

Among the Germanic people, the "700" is sometimes "the largest in the range of 7".

The "800"

b) traditional-mythological symbolism of the "800"

The Hebrew letter "Pe" represents a mouth. Pe is primarily the number "80", but is also used for the "800".

c) system symbolism of the "800"

Among the Germanic peoples, the "800" is sometimes "the greatest in the range of 8", that is, "the greatest in the range of perfection". This generally means something related to the "perfect sun", i.e. Tyr.

The "900"

b) traditional-mythological symbolism of the "900"

The Hebrew letter "Tzade" (Tzadi) represents a papyrus or generally a plant, but is also understood as a harpoon. This symbolic character for the "90" is also used for the "900".

c) system symbolism of the "900"

With the Teutons the "900" is sometimes "the largest in the range of the 9". For example, the goddess ("100") of the otherworld ("9") has $9 \cdot 100 = 900$ heads.

The "1000"

b) traditional-mythological symbolism of the "1000"

In the decimal system the "1000" is the "very large number". This symbolism is also found among the Germanic peoples.

The "1001"

b) traditional-mythological symbolism of the "1001"

In the Arabic area the "1001" has the meaning "even more than very many". This is probably best known by the title "alf leila wa-leila", i.e. "Thousand and one Nights".

Similarly, in the European area there is the old saying "after a year and a day", i.e. "even later on as one year". This idiom is also based on the image of "more than the very great number".

The "1,000,000"

b) traditional-mythological symbolism of the "1,000,000"

In the decimal system, the "1000" is the "incredibly large number". This symbolism is also found among the Egyptians: The boat of the sun was called "boat of millions of years", i.e. "the boat that crosses the sky in eternity".

English Books by Harry Eilenstein

- Living Magic (261 p.)
- The Synthesis of Physics and Magic (192 p.)
- Astral Projection for Beginners (60 p.)
- Invocations for Beginners (52 p.)
- Evocations for Beginners (62 p.)
- Auto-Movement for Beginners (60 p.)
- Elves for Beginners (56 p.)
- Hypnosis for Beginners (56 p.)
- Shamanism for Beginners (52 p.)
- Crop Circles for Beginners (344 p.)
- Number Symbolism for Beginners (64 p.)

These books will be puplished soon:

- Telepathy for Beginners
- Telepathy for Advanced Learners
- Telekinesis for Beginners
- Life Force for Beginners
- Meditation for Beginners
- Kundalini for Beginners

- Chakra-Magic for Beginners
- Astrology for Beginners
- Ritual Magic for Beginners
- Mandalas for Beginners
- Money Magic for Beginners
- Love Magic for Beginners
- Magic Research for Beginners
- Self-awareness for Beginners
- Symbolism of Numbers for Beginners
- Language of the Moon – for Beginners
- Magic Chant for Beginners
- Prophecy for Beginners
- Magic Objects for Beginners
- Da'ath-Magic for Beginners
- Feng Shui for Beginners
- Magic for Beginners – Anthology I
- Magic for Beginners – Anthology II
- Magic for Beginners – Anthology III
- Magic for Beginners – Anthology IV

Bücher von Harry Eilenstein

Religion allgemein
- Die sieben Schritte des Lebens (428 S.)
- Muttergöttin und Schamanen (168 S.)
- Göbekli Tepe (472 S.)
- Die Göttin von Göbekli Tepe (144 S.)
- Totempfähle (440 S.)
- Christus (60 S.)
- Dakini (80 S.)
- Vajra (76 S.)

Ägypten
- Hathor und Re 1: Götter und Mythen im Alten Ägypten (432 S.)
- Hathor und Re 2: Die altägyptische Religion – Ursprünge, Kult und Magie (396 S.)
- Isis (508 S.)

Indogermanen
- Die Entwicklung der indogermanischen Religionen (700 S.)
- Wurzeln und Zweige der indogermanischen Religion (224 S.)

Germanen
- Die Götter der Germanen (87 Bände – siehe nächste Seite)
- Odin (300 S.)

Kelten
- Cernunnos (690 S.)
- Taliesin (228 S.)
- Der Kessel von Gundestrup (220 S.)
- Der Chiemsee-Kessel (76)

Psychologie
- Über die Freude (100 S.)
- Das Geheimnis des inneren Friedens (252 S.)
- Das Beziehungsmandala (52 S.)
- Gefühle und ihre Verwandlungen (404 S.)
- einsgerichtet (140 S.)
- Liebe und Eigenständigkeit (216 S.)
- Von innerer Fülle zu äußerem Gedeihen (52 S.)

Heilung
- Die Symbolik der Krankheiten (76 S.)

Kunst
- Herz des Tanzes – Tanz des Herzens (160 S.)

Drama
- König Athelstan (104 S.)

Bücher von Harry Eilenstein

„Magie für Anfänger"	**Magie**
- Telepathie für Anfänger (60 S.)	- Handbuch für Zauberlehrlinge (408 S.)
- Telepathie für Fortgeschrittene (52 S.)	- Tarot (104 S.)
- Telekinese für Anfänger (52 S.)	- Physik und Magie (184 S.)
- Lebenskraft für Anfänger (60 S.)	- Die Synthese von Physik und Magie (200S.)
- Meditation für Anfänger (56 S.)	- Die Magie-Formel (156 S.)
- Kundalini für Anfänger (100 S.)	- Krafttiere – Tiergöttinnen – Tiertänze (112 S.)
- Hypnose für Anfänger (56 S.)	- Schwitzhütten (524 S.)
- Auto-Movement für Anfänger (56 S.)	- Mythen und Magie der Harfe (116 S.)
- Chakra-Magie für Anfänger (148 S.)	- Magie heute – Berichte aus der Praxis (288 S.)
- Astralreisen für Anfänger (56 S.)	**Meditation**
- Astrologie für Anfänger (120 S.)	- Der Lebenskraftkörper (230 S.)
- Ritual-Magie für Anfänger (56 S.)	- Die Chakren (100 S.)
- Mandalas für Anfänger (68 S.)	- Das Chakren-System mit den Nebenchakren
- Geldzauber für Anfänger (56 S.)	(296 S.)
- Liebeszauber für Anfänger (52 S.)	- Organe und Chakren (64 S.)
- Invokationen für Anfänger (52 S.)	- Die platonischen Körper in den Chakren (156 S.)
- Evokationen für Anfänger (60 S.)	- Meditation (140 S.)
- Elfen für Anfänger (56 S.)	- Drachenfeuer (124 S.)
- Magie-Forschung für Anfänger (140 S.)	- Kundalini I (676 S.)
- Selbsterkenntnis für Anfänger (52 S.)	- Reinkarnation (156 S.)
- Zahlensymbolik für Anfänger (60 S.)	- einsgerichtet (140 S.)
- Die Sprache des Mondes – für Anfänger (116 S.)	**Astrologie**
- Zaubergesänge für Anfänger (100 S.)	- Astrologie (496 S.)
- Zukunftschau für Anfänger (60 S.)	- Photo-Astrologie (428 S.)
- Schamanismus für Anfänger (52 S.)	- Die astrologischen Aspekte (88 S.)
- Magische Gegenstände für Anfänger (68 S.)	- Horoskop und Seele (120 S.)
- Da'ath-Magie für Anfänger (64 S.)	**Kabbala**
- Kornkreise für Anfänger (348 S.)	- Kursus der praktischen Kabbala (150 S.)
- Feng Shui für Anfänger (96 S.)	- Eltern der Erde (450 S.)
- Magie für Anfänger – Sammelband I (696 S.)	- Blüten des Lebensbaumes:
- Magie für Anfänger – Sammelband II (664 S.)	- Die Struktur des kabbalistischen
- Magie für Anfänger – Sammelband III (580 S.)	Lebensbaumes (370 S.)
„Traumreisen"	- Der kabbalistische Lebensbaum als
- Traumreisen zu Heilpflanzen (700 S.)	Forschungshilfsmittel (580 S.)
	- Der kabbalistische Lebensbaum als
	spirituelle Landkarte (520 S.)

Die Themen der 87 Bände der Reihe „Die Götter der Germanen"

1. Die Entwicklung der germanischen Religion
2. Lexikon der germanischen Religion
3. Der ursprüngliche Göttervater Tyr
4. Tyr in der Unterwelt: der Schmied Wieland
5. Tyr in der Unterwelt: der Riesenkönig   Teil 1
6. Tyr in der Unterwelt: der Riesenkönig   Teil 2
7. Tyr in der Unterwelt: der Zwergenkönig
8. Der Himmelswächter Heimdall
9. Der Sommergott Baldur
10. Der Meeresgott: Ägir, Hler und Njörd
11. Der Eibengott Ullr
12. Die Zwillingsgötter Alcis
13. Der neue Göttervater Odin   Teil 1
14. Der neue Göttervater Odin   Teil 2
15. Der Fruchtbarkeitsgott Freyr
16. Der Chaos-Gott Loki
17. Der Donnergott Thor
18. Der Priestergott Hönir
19. Die Göttersöhne
20. Die unbekannteren Götter
21. Die Göttermutter Frigg
22. Die Liebesgöttin: Freya und Menglöd
23. Die Erdgöttinnen
24. Die Korngöttin Sif
25. Die Apfel-Göttin Idun
26. Die Hügelgrab-Jenseitsgöttin Hel
27. Die Meeres-Jenseitsgöttin Ran
28. Die unbekannteren Jenseitsgöttinnen
29. Die unbekannteren Göttinnen
30. Die Nornen
31. Die Walküren
32. Die Zwerge
33. Der Urriese Ymir
34. Die Riesen
35. Die Riesinnen
36. Mythologische Wesen
37. Mythologische Priester und Priesterinnen
38. Sigurd/Siegfried
39. Helden und Göttersöhne
40. Die Symbolik der Vögel und Insekten
41. Die Symbolik der Schlangen, Drachen und Ungeheuer
42.a Die Symbolik der Herdentiere I
42.b Die Symbolik der Herdentiere II
43. Die Symbolik der Raubtiere
44. Die Symbolik der Wassertiere und sonstigen Tiere
45. Die Symbolik der Pflanzen
46. Die Symbolik der Farben
47. Die Symbolik der Zahlen
48. Die Symbolik von Sonne, Mond und Sternen
49.a Das Jenseits I – Das Hügelgrab
49.b Das Jenseits II – Der Jenseitsweg
50. Seelenvogel, Utiseta und Einweihung
51. Wiederzeugung und Wiedergeburt
52. Elemente der Kosmologie
53. Der Weltenbaum
54. Die Symbolik der Himmelsrichtungen und der Jahreszeiten
55.a Mythologische Motive I
55.b Mythologische Motive II
56. Der Tempel
57. Die Einrichtung des Tempels
58. Priesterin – Seherin – Zauberin – Hexe
59. Priester – Seher – Zauberer
60. Rituelle Kleidung und Schmuck
61. Skalden und Skaldinnen
62 Kriegerinnen und Ekstase-Krieger
63. Die Symbolik der Körperteile
64.a Magie und Ritual I
64.b Magie und Ritual II
64.c Magie und Ritual III
65. Gestaltwandlungen
66.a Magische Angriffs-Waffen
66.b Magische Verteidigungs-Waffen
67. Magische Werkzeuge und Gegenstände
68. Zaubersprüche
69. Göttermet
70. Zaubertränke
71. Träume, Omen und Orakel
72. Runen
73. Sozial-religiöse Rituale
74. Weisheiten und Sprichworte
75. Kenningar
76. Rätsel
77. Die vollständige Edda des Snorri Sturluson
78. Frühe Skaldenlieder
79.a Mythologische Sagas I
79.b Mythologische Sagas II
80. Hymnen an die germanischen Götter